Backup Dobro

Exploring the Fretboard
By Doug Cox

In this book you'll learn creative, fun techniques and ideas on playing backup. Playing backup means responding in a sensitive manner with singers and other musicians. So, lets take a serious look at what to do when you're not soloing. The question is: To play? or not to play?

Cover Photo - Chris Manuel
Cover Guitar – Rayco Resophonic
CD Recorded at Windswept Media
Engineered - Chris Manuel
Cover Art - Shawn Brown
Notation - George Ports
Production – Ron Middlebrook

ISBN 1-57424-133-8
SAN 683-8022

Table of Contents and CD Track List

Doug Cox Bio

From his home in the Comox Valley on Vancouver Island, BC, Doug Cox has carved-out an amazingly diverse career as a teacher, recording artist and touring musician. He has played festivals, clubs and concert halls across Canada, the United States and around the world. From Dobrofest in Slovakia; to performances in the Yukon; to the Baseball Hall of Fame in Cooperstown, New York, Cox's unique musical journey continues in many 'roots' music veins. For information on Doug's recordings, tour dates and other instructional materials visit www.dougcox.org.

Introduction

The house lights go down and the audience goes quiet. The curtain goes up and a single super-trooper spotlight shines on a lone guitar player who strums a brief intro into a song. He is joined by other instruments as each bar of music builds until the singer steps in and grabs the spotlight triumphantly with the first few notes of singing.

Dramatic, isn't it? You can enhance the drama or destroy it simply by what you choose to do as a player in those first few notes played. *"To play or not to play"...* that is the question. As a painter paints a background to bring out the subtleties of his subject, so should you strive to create a suitable backdrop for the lead instrument or vocal in every situation. Too much purple will draw attention away from the Mona Lisa's eyes.

As a great chef creates a sauce that brings out the flavors of his main course, so should you add to the jumbo of a good backup band. Too much hot sauce will kill the taste buds and wilt the peppers. As a great comedian delivers the final punch line with impeccable timing so should you save the sparkle for the right moments. Too fast or too loud or too much is only that; *too fast, too loud and too much!* The master magician or athlete never shows you what they are capable of just so you can marvel at how long they have practiced their craft... all magic appears effortless. *Get the point?*

O.K., away from philosophy and back to basics! This book series will look at various Dobro techniques including explorations of *rhythm, harmony, bass lines, arpeggios and counter point.* Most of your playing time will be spent as a backup player so it only makes sense to take a serious *(but fun!)* look at what you are doing when not soloing. That will be the focus of this series... creative, fun techniques and ideas for the modern Dobro player, encompassing many styles of roots music. You will benefit most from this book if you start from the beginning and work your way through, chapter by chapter. However, if you are an intermediate or advanced player, you may want to skim through the book and find sections that will advance your playing immediately.

Spend some time listening to great backup players in all styles of music. Listen to what each instrument does when it's not playing the lead role. Listen to horn sections and organ players. Listen to drummers and bass players. Listen to mandolin and banjo players. Listen to string sections. Listen to backup vocalists. Imagine yourself as any one of those things when you are playing the Dobro, it'll lead you into many new ways of playing. Remember, playing *backup* means responding in a sensitive manner to what is going on. Most of all...*listen!*

Tuning

(Track 1)
We will use the standard Dobro (Lap Style) tuning throughout this book.
This tuning, from low string to high string is GBDGBD.

Understanding the Major Scale

The easiest way to understand music theory is to have a good grasp on how the piano keyboard works. This is because all the notes on the keyboard are laid out in a very linear fashion, simply repeating themselves, over and over.

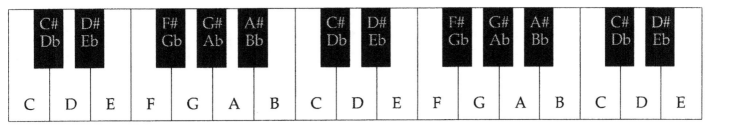

Take note of the fact that each black key has two names.
Take note of the fact that there is no black key between the E & F notes and the B & C notes.

We are going to spend most of our time in this book looking at the key of G major because the Dobro is tuned to a G chord. However, the easiest key to understand on the keyboard is C major because it uses only the white keys on the piano. In other words, there are no flats (b) or sharps (#) in the key of C major. If you ever get confused about music theory, just go back to the Key of C major and analyze things from there!

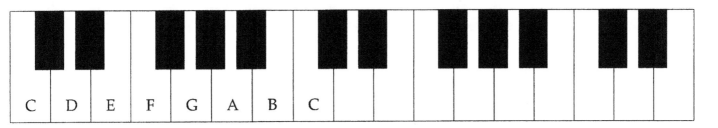

All major scales follow the same formula. Lets count the number of steps required to make a C major scale on the keyboard.

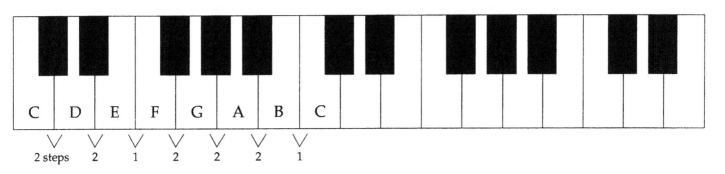

As you can see, the formula for the C major scale (starting on C and counting up) is 2 steps, 2 steps, 1 step, 2 steps, 2 steps, 2 steps, 1 step. On the Dobro, (or any other fretted instrument) this simply means 2 frets, 2 frets, 1 fret, 2 frets, 2 frets, 2 frets, 1 fret.

Another way you may encounter this formula uses the terms tone and semitone. A tone means 2 steps. A semitone means 1 step. So here's another look at the major scale formula using tones, steps, or frets.

Tone,	Tone,	Semitone,	Tone,	Tone,	Tone,	Semitone	or
2 steps	2 steps	1 step	2 steps	2 steps	2 steps	1 step	or
2 frets	2 frets	1 fret	2 frets	2 frets	2 frets	1 fret	

Try starting anywhere on your instrument and play the above formula on one string. Your ears should tell you that you are playing a major scale !

Now lets look at the G major scale. You can see that it follows the same formula as C major.

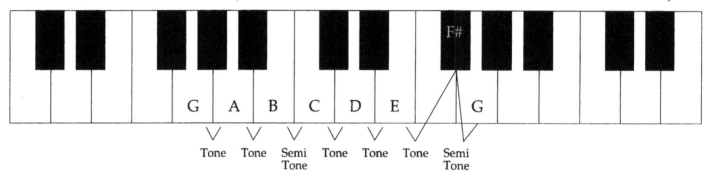

We are going to use 'scale degrees' instead of 'note names' for most of this book. The reason for this is that the relationships between notes never change no matter what key you are in...just the note names do. Thinking in terms of note names instead of scale degrees just complicates things! The only reason we need note names is to give us a reference point as to where we start. Here is the G major scale using scale degrees instead of note names.

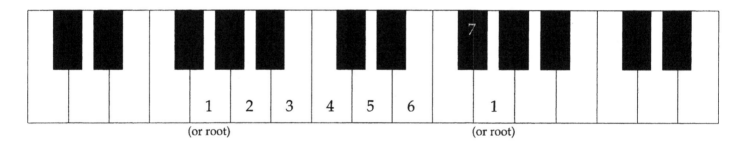

For comparison sake, here's the C major scale using scale degrees.

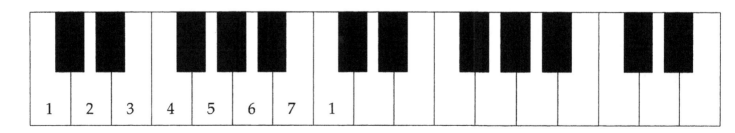

...see how they are both the same thing? All the major scales work this way.

Basic I, IV, V (1, 4, 5) Chord Progressions

In every style of music you will encounter the I, IV, V chord progression. Musicians will often say things like, " it's in the key of A and starts on the V " or, " Key of G from the I ". You need to be able to decipher this language in order to jam with them. Here's how you do it.

The I chord is the 'root or name' of the key. The I chord in the Key of G is G. To figure out the IV, just count up four letter names on your fingers . The IV chord in the Key of G is C. (count up 4...G, A, B, C)
The V is one up from the IV. In the key of G that's D. (G, A, B, C, D...count 'em!)
That's all there is to it!

Track 3

Key (I)	IV	V
G	C	D
Open	5 Fret	7 Fret

Key (I)	IV	V
A	D	E
2 Fret	7 Fret	9 Fret

Key (I)	IV	V
E	A	B
9 Fret	2 Fret	4 Fret

Key (I)	IV	V
C	F	G
5 Fret	10 Fret	12 Fret

Key (I)	IV	V
D	G	A
7 Fret	Open	2 Fret

The I, IV, V is the most used chord progression. As a backup Dobro player you will have to find interesting but unobtrusive things to play over all the keys using this progression. It is imperative that you are able to find the I, IV and V chords in whatever key you are playing in. It's also very fun and useful to memorize licks (a lick is a musical phrase) that will lead you from one chord into the next...but more on that later.

Dobro Neck Major Chords

The great thing about using the open G tuning is that by simply playing the open strings or laying your bar down across the neck you are playing a major chord. That's not how it works in standard guitar tuning!

Here are the major chord bar positions for the Dobro.

G (open strings)	G# or Ab	A	A# or Bb	B	C	C# or Db	D	D# or Eb	E	F	F# or Gb	G	R	e	p	e	a

To play in tune, you want to play right over the top of the fret markers on the Dobro. Playing below the markers you will be flat and above you will be sharp. Remember to play on TOP of the fret.

The enclosed CD has an exercise for practicing playing the I, IV, V chord progression in all the above keys. If you haven't mastered this, go to the CD now and play with the I, IV, V tracks in the above keys until you are comfortable with them. Note how I am damping the strings on the recording for the 'chick' part of the boom-chick sound. This is done by raising the bar off the strings and leaving the fingers behind the bar (left hand) down on the strings. See photo below.

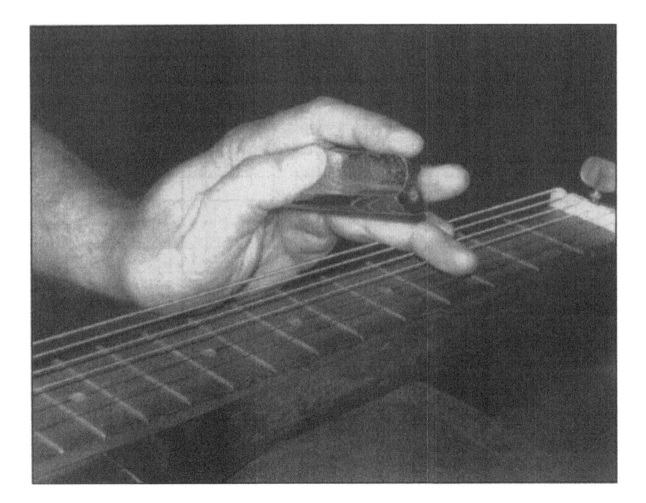

Our Buddy... G Major

G major is the most popular key for Dobro players because the Dobro is tuned to two G major chords.

G Major Scale

I (root)	ii (second)	iii (third)	IV(fourth)	V (fifth)	Vi (sixth)	Vii (seventh)	I (root)
G	A	B	C	D	E	F#	G

The major chord is made up of three notes within the major scale, the root, third and fifth. In the Key of G, they are G, B and D. Lets look at the Dobro tuning.

$$1st \ string \ = D \ (fifth)$$
$$2^{nd} \ string \ = B \ (third)$$
$$3^{rd} \ string \ = G \ (root)$$
$$4^{th} \ string \ = D \ (fifth)$$
$$5^{th} \ string \ = B \ (third)$$
$$6^{th} \ string \ = G \ (root)$$

As you can see, the Dobro tuning consists of the notes that make up two G chords. This means all the open strings fit safely into the Key of G, making G the safest key to play in.

Backup playing includes counter-melody lines (responding to what the singer or lead instrument plays) and bass lines. This means a good working knowledge of the Dobro neck is needed. To accomplish this...you guessed it ...*scales are needed.*

My approach to music theory has been to thoroughly learn and understand the major scale. I can then twist and contort the major scale into all other scales, intervals and chords.
So...even though this is a 'backup' book and not a 'lead' book, we still need to know the scales. Constant daily (slow!!) repetition is an effective practice method towards progressing with scale and roll patterns.

*** PRACTICE TIP – SLOW DOWN!! PRACTICE SLOWER THAN YOU NEED TO AND EXPERIMENT WITH YOUR TONE, VIBRATO AND INTONATION (PITCH). IT IS HELPFUL TO ACTUALLY MAKE A SIGN THAT SAYS 'SLOW DOWN' AND PUT IT ON YOUR MUSIC STAND OR UP ON THE WALL WHERE YOU PRACTICE. REMEMBER, IF YOU CAN'T PLAY IT SLOW, YOU CAN'T PLAY IT FAST.

SLOW DOWN

Memorize the following 6 scales. They will prove to be very useful in your future playing! Play each scale up and down, from top to bottom and from bottom to top.

G scale 1

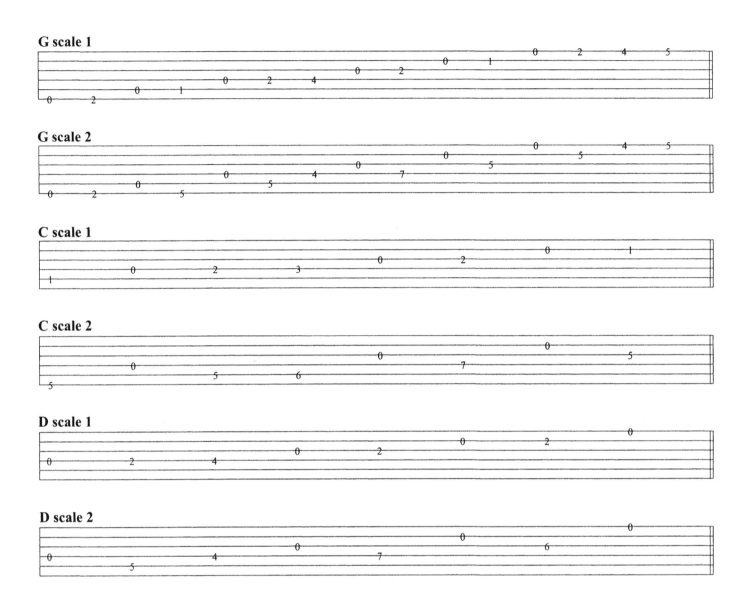

G scale 2

C scale 1

C scale 2

D scale 1

D scale 2

Once you have memorized a scale pattern, see if you can pick out the notes of a very simple melody by ear. For example, try the old favorite 'Three Blind Mice'...a song that is played at most jam sessions (yeah right!) ...I'll give you a hint; in the key of G the song starts with a B note, or your open 2nd or 5th string. The ability to pick out melodies by ear is a very important skill if you wish to be a back-up player. If you are having trouble telling what direction to move in as you go from note to note than sing the melody and see if you can physically feel which direction the notes are moving in. Don't get frustrated if this is new to you, practice will make you better.

Running Scales Together

Now we are going to take the three scales and run them together through a I, IV, V chord progression. A tip to effective practice sessions is to learn a little bit at a time. If you are running the G, C and D scales together, make sure you have the G pattern memorized before you add the C pattern . Once you have memorized the G pattern and the C pattern, pay particular attention to the transition between the two scales.   Smooth transitions between scales or melodic ideas show attention to detail and clean playing. Remember, backup playing is largely improvisation. In other words, you are not going to play a memorized song when you are backing someone else up. You are going to make use of memorized scales, licks, arpeggios and patterns. What this means is that if you don't actually learn (memorize) the information in this book, than you won't be able to use it while backing someone up. Think of it as your language; you can't stop and look words up in the dictionary if you are going to use them to express yourself, you have to have them down! So pick the patterns you really like and make them part of you.

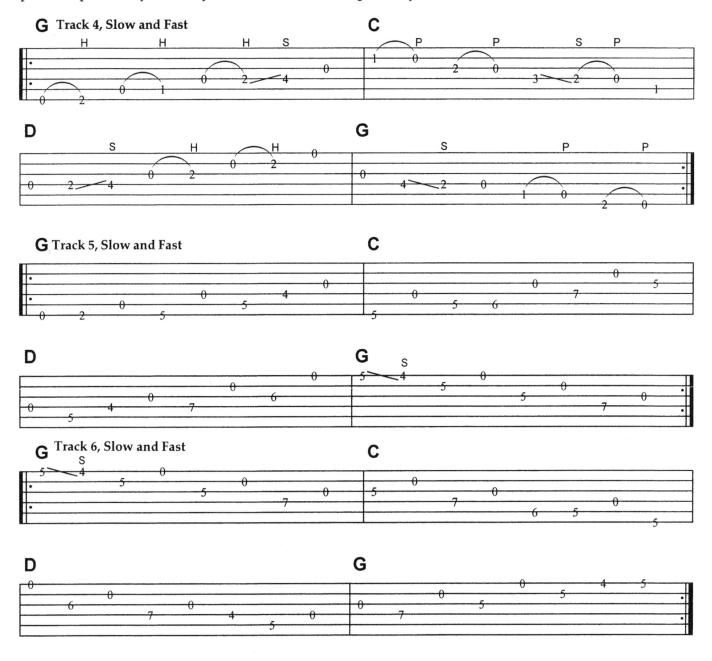

...see if you can come up with your own ways to run the scales together.

Descending Octaves

Counterpoint is when you answer a lead melody or voice with a different but complimentary melody. Jerry Douglas and Sally Van Meter are absolute masters at this style of Dobro playing. This can happen underneath the lead voice or it can fill in the space right after the lead voice. One great sound for backup counterpoint playing is the octave sound.

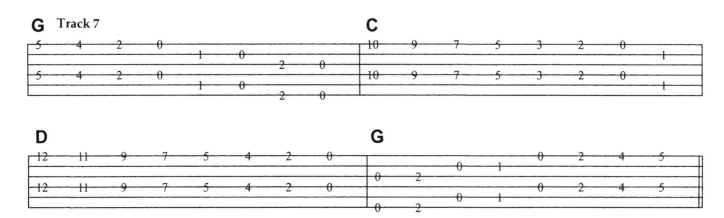

Jerry Douglas and Sally Van Meter
Courtesy of the Strawberry Music Festival
Visit Sally at: www.sallyvanmeter.com

I like to practice all scales in '3s', meaning: go up 3 notes, come back one note and go up three more notes. This will help with your phrasing so you're not always playing your scales just straight up and down. Take the same concept and play 4's, 5s, 6s, etc.

G

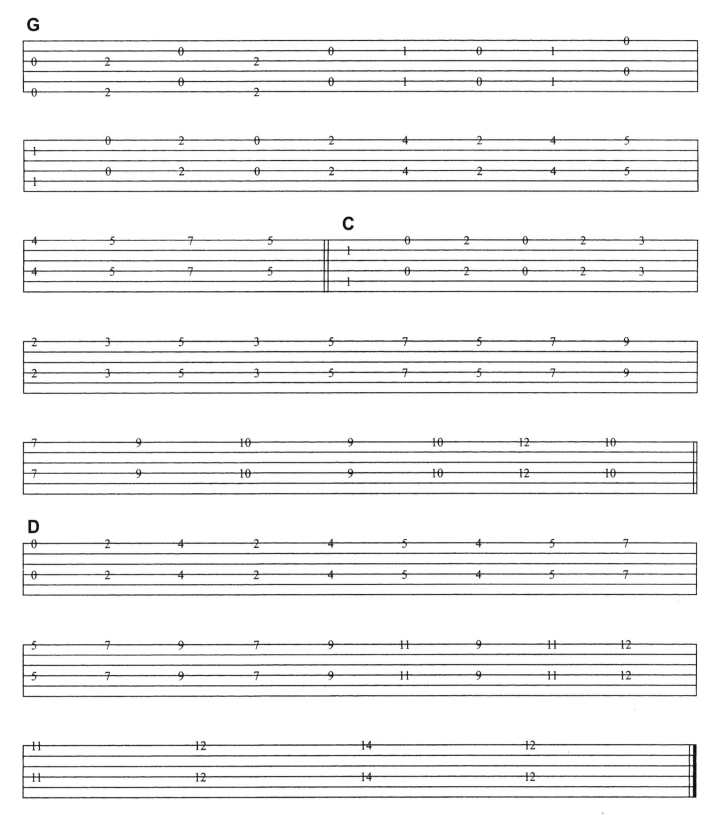

C

D

Try the following D scale, in 3s, on your top string only. Only allow yourself to pick the string once and then play all other notes by sliding up and down the string without picking the string again with your left hand. This is fun and it's very good for your intonation. If you have a dog or cat, it will drive them crazy as well but be careful, even Fluffy and Rover can only take so much of a good thing!

Practicing scales in as many patterns as possible is a great way to insure when your moment comes as a backup player, that you can pull off whichever phrase you wish to play. Here's another great practice pattern for all your scales; this pattern has you skip a note every step of the way.

Scales

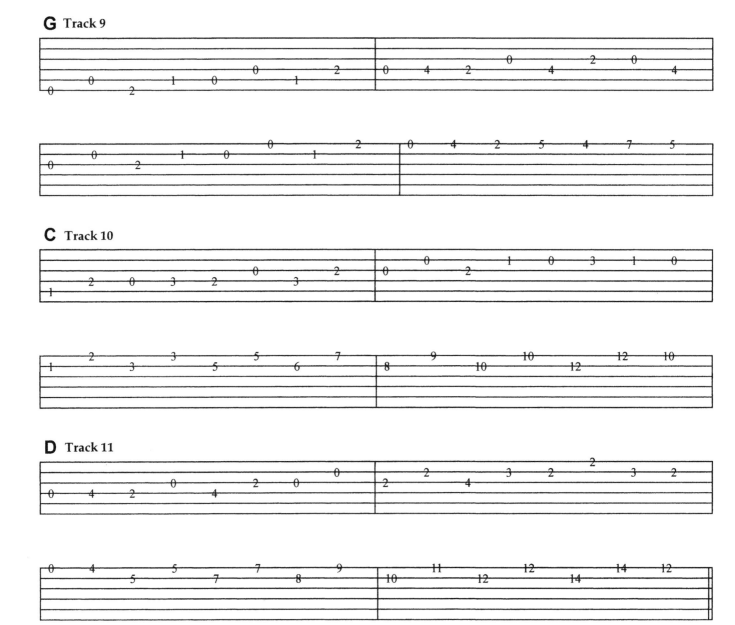

14

Arpeggios

Arpeggios are notes that make up chords, played separately instead of all at once. For example, if you strum across the 1st, 2nd and 3rd strings than you are playing a G chord. If you play each of those strings separately, than you are playing a G major arpeggio. If you are confused about this, listen to the recorded example on your CD,

Further Explanation : there are a few terms you should understand to grasp the concepts of melody and harmony. Have a look at the general definitions for the following words ...

Note: One sound or string on your instrument played in a singular fashion
Melody: A run of single notes played one after the other creating a memorable phrase
Interval: The relationship between two notes played together
Chord: 3 or more notes played together
Arpeggio: The notes that make up a specific chord played separately or if you like, in a melodic fashion.

The study of harmony is another book (at least!) in itself but is a crucial element to the development of your musical skills! To start, try to figure out which of the above components are being used in some of your favorite music. This will increase the depth of your listening skills and eventually, your playing will follow.

Different types of chords are made up of different notes within the scale. To understand the arpeggio patterns we are going to play, we need to learn the 3 major scale patterns we are going to build our arpeggios from. *"Why are we learning 3 patterns for one scale,"* you moan? Well Dobro fans, it's because we want to be able to start our approach in any key from any of the 6 strings on the Dobro. We will learn the patterns beginning from where the root notes are located on each of the 6 strings.

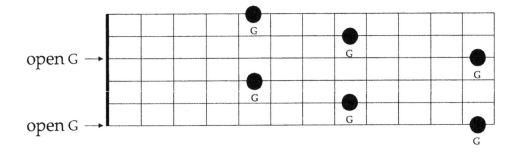

As you can see from this diagram, learning a major scale that relates to each root note location will allow us to play from any location on the neck instead of being stuck in one place! Practice playing all your G notes on the Dobro until you can find them with ease.

3 Visual Patterns

Take a look at the scales below using three visual forms. Don't get confused into thinking you are looking at different things, they are all the same. There is a good reason for understanding each of the three ways the scale is presented...

1. <u>Visual pattern</u> – this is so you can see the 'shape' of the pattern without anything else getting in the way. Take a good look at the shape and then close your eyes... now see if you can visualize the shape of the scale in your mind. This is a great way to speed up the memorization process. It's also a good way of testing yourself. If you can't see the pattern with your eyes closed, than you don't really know it.

G (I)   G Scale

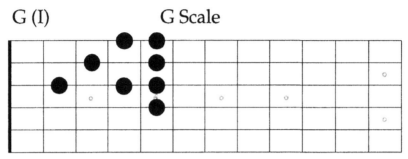

Try practicing visualizing these shapes without your Dobro in hand as often as you can. This is a good thing to do while waiting for a bus, when TV commercials are on, or instead of counting sheep while trying to go to sleep. Warning... do not do this while operating heavy machinery or while in conversation with your significant other!

2. <u>Tablature pattern</u> – this allows you to think of the specific location on the fretboard for the particular scale you are playing; in this case, G major.

3. <u>Scale Degrees</u> – once you have memorized the pattern, than you need to know the scale degree you are playing with each note. This is how you manipulate your major scale into arpeggios and other scales. Your scale degrees are the root, second, third, fourth, fifth, sixth and seventh as listed below...

G Major Scale

I (root)	ii (second)	iii (third)	IV(fourth)	V (fifth)	Vi (sixth)	Vii (seventh)	I (root)
G	A	B	C	D	E	F#	G

Practice techniques for mastering the scale patterns

Play the pattern up and down.
Play the pattern using the 'skipping note' technique as we did with the previous scale exercise.
Once you have mastered the pattern, practice your scale while saying out loud the degree of the scale you are playing. Then, test yourself by playing the root and then the third, the root and then the fifth, the root and then the fourth, etc.
Once you can do all the above, it is safe to say you know the pattern and you will be able to start working with it !

Now we are going to take the same scale pattern and move it through the I, IV, V chord progression in the key of G major.

Pattern: G C D G G C D G

Track 13

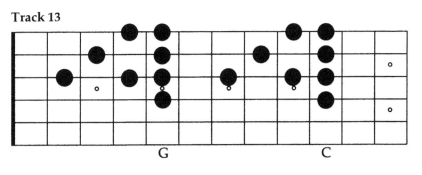

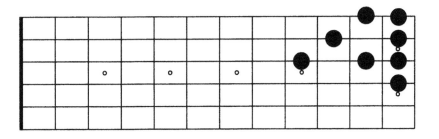

David Nance

Next, we are going to move onto the second scale pattern with the root notes on the 2nd and 5th strings. Use the same practice techniques to memorize this pattern as you did on the last.

Visual

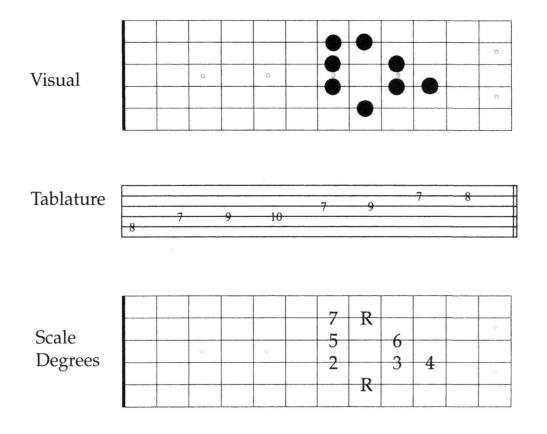

Tablature

Scale
Degrees

We will repeat the same exercises for this pattern as the 1st pattern. The chord progression is: G C D G G C D G.

Track 14

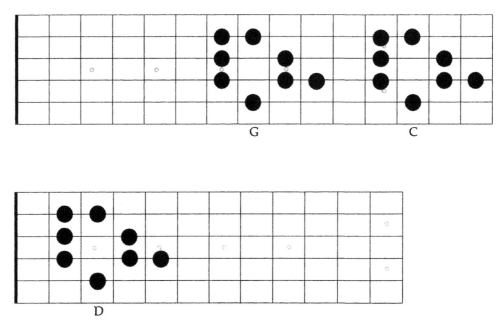

Here comes the third scale pattern with the root notes on the 3rd and 6th strings. Once again, use the same practice techniques to memorize this pattern as you did on previous ones.

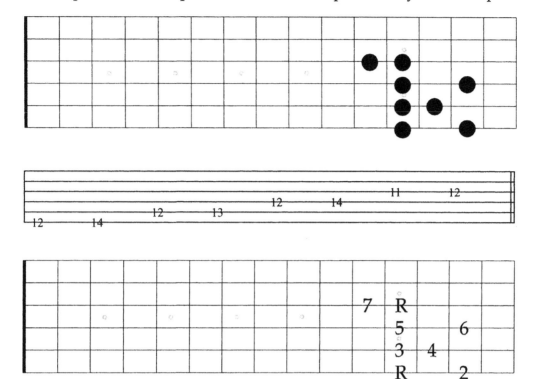

We will repeat the same exercises for this pattern as the others.
The chord progression is: G C D G G C D G.

Track 15

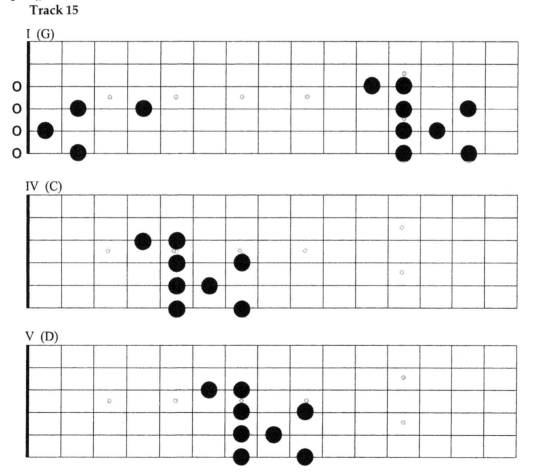

note - using this pattern, we can play two octaves of the G scale, one uses the open strings as demonstrated on the CD. The other starts on the 12th fret.

Lets look at all three patterns together on one page for the key of G.

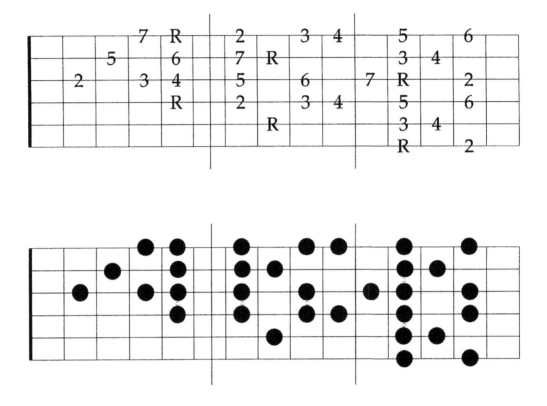

You should be able to see how these patterns tie
together up and down the neck of your instrument.

Paula Jones

How the scales tie together using the I IV V chords

Lets look at how the major scales that are related to the I , IV and V chords relate to each other in the different positions we have learned. Have a look at the following patterns and do the exercises for each pattern on your CD. Pattern: G C D G G C D G

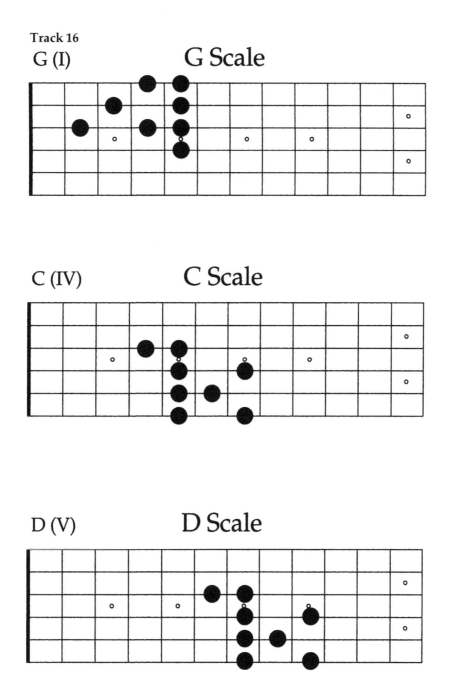

Track 16

G (I)   G Scale

C (IV)   C Scale

D (V)   D Scale

note - when playing over the V chord of a major key, (D in the key of G), you will eventually play the flat 7th of the scale that relates to the V chord. This is an important distinction to make and something we will touch on later in this series. For now, we will continue to work on our major scale patterns.

Pattern G C D G G C D G

G (I)   ## G Scale

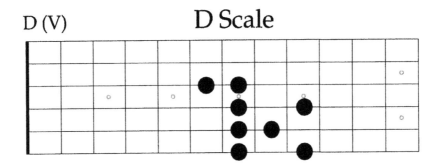

C (IV)   ## C Scale

D (V)   ## D Scale

Paul Beard and Josh Graves
with "Josh Graves" model guitar

Pattern G C D G G C D G

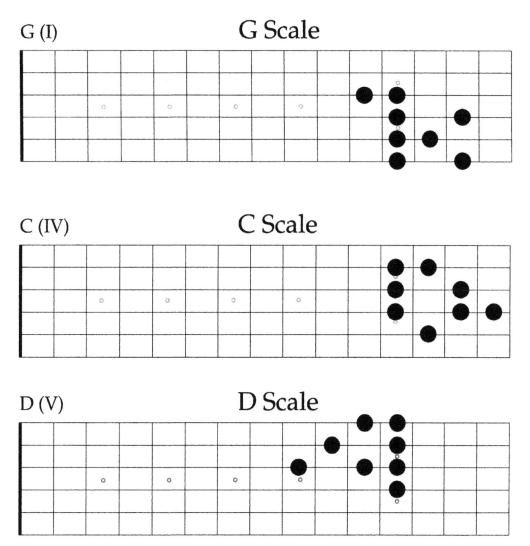

G (I) **G Scale**

C (IV) **C Scale**

D (V) **D Scale**

You will find while playing the exercises above, that some patterns run together more comfortably than others. Some are very awkward. Every player seems to have his/her favorite spots on the instrument to play and you have to find yours. This is one of the things that gives each of us our own unique voice on the Dobro.

*I have learned as a teacher that each student sees things in a different way. There are many different ways to present information. Some of us have strong visual learning abilities while for others its physical or aural (hearing) abilities that are strongest. Some of us see patterns clearly while others think in more esoteric ways. It is a real challenge to figure out how a student thinks and how to impart information to individual students in a way they might easily understand. As a student, you should try to figure out your strong points of understanding and then take any learning information you may have and if you need to, translate it into the language that you works best for you.

Patterns Above and Below each Root Note

We could go on looking at patterns forever! I am going to present you with two more ways of looking at the Dobro neck in regards to scale patterns and then we will move on.

So far, we have looked at only one pattern that fits around each root note. Another way to look at the neck is to try the patterns that fit above and below each root note. In doing this, you will find there is almost always a comfortable way to move throughout the neck…you just have to find it!

Root note on 1st and 4th strings

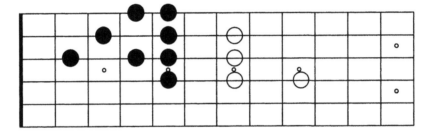

Pattern below root notes

Pattern above root notes

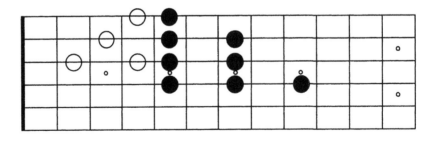

Root note on 2nd and 5th string

Pattern below root notes

Pattern above root notes

Root note on 3rd and 6th strings

Pattern below root notes

Pattern above root notes

Now, for reference sake, lets take a look at the Dobro neck naming all the notes on the Dobro.

Fretboard Notes

	Eb	E	F	Gb	G	Ab	A	Bb	B	C	Db	D
D												
B	C	Db	D	Eb	E	F	Gb	G	Ab	A	Bb	B
G	Ab	A	Bb	B	C	Db	D	Eb	E	F	Gb	G
D	Eb	E	F	Gb	G	Ab	A	Bb	B	C	Db	D
B	C	Db	D	Eb	E	F	Gb	G	Ab	A	Bb	B
G	Ab	A	Bb	B	C	Db	D	Eb	E	F	Gb	G

…and the scale degrees for the key of G throughout the Dobro neck.

	#5	6	b7	7	R	b2	2	b3	3	4	b5	5
5												
3	4	b5	5	#5	6	b7	7	R	b2	2	b3	3
R	b2	2	b3	3	4	b5	5	#5	6	b7	7	R
5	#5	6	b7	7	R	b2	2	b3	3	4	b5	5
3	4	b5	5	#5	6	b7	7	R	b2	2	b3	3
R	b2	2	b3	3	4	b5	5	#5	6	b7	7	R

Scale degrees will lead us into chord arpeggios as that is what they are made of.

Arpeggios

Here are the simple formulas for making up major, minor and 7th chords. In this case each chord is led out using the root note of G. Don't get overwhelmed by this chart or why it's in this book. You will in to understand it once we start playing arpeggios. It's all just part of the path towards understanding sic. Every type of chord has a very distinct personality that you will begin to recognize. Every style of sic has it's own rules about which type of chords are used that help to define that style. In this book, we going to cover major, minor and 7th chords.

G Major Scale

I (root)	ii (second)	iii (third)	IV(fourth)	V (fifth)	Vi (sixth)	Vii (seventh)	I (root)
G	A	B	C	D	E	F#	G

Chord Construction Chart

Major Chord (G major)

R - G
3rd - B
5th ⁻ D

Minor Chord (G minor)
(minor means flat the 3rd
in relation to the major scale)

R - G
b3rd - Bb
5th ⁻ D

Major 7th Chord (GMaj 7)
(the only time you use the 7th
within the major scale is when
the chord is called a <u>Major 7th</u> chord)!

R - G
3rd ⁻ B
5th ⁻ D
7th ⁻ F#

Dominant 7th or 7th Chord
(the 'blues' 7th chord) (G7)

R - G
3rd ⁻ B
5th ⁻ D
7th ⁻ F

Minor 7th Chord
(remember, minor means flat 3rd)

R - G
3rd ⁻ Bb
5th ⁻ D
b7th - F

3 Major Arpeggio Shapes

Now let's put all this theory to work on the Dobro.
Here are the 3 Major arpeggio shapes on the Dobro neck.

G Major Arpeggios

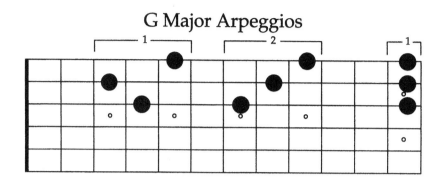

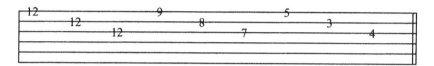

Leroy McNees

Lets play through these major arpeggios.

Of course, we can do the same thing on the bass strings.

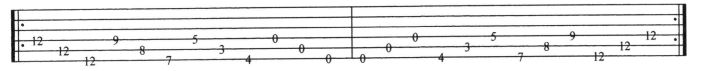

Lets play through the I, IV, V progression in the key of G using each of the three arpeggios shapes as a starting point and moving into the closest shape we can for each chord. You should be able to see the incredible potential of knowing your arpeggios!

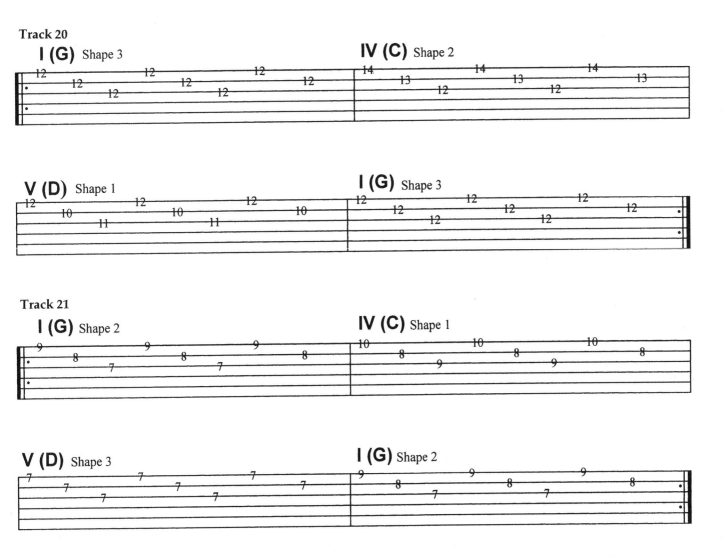

29

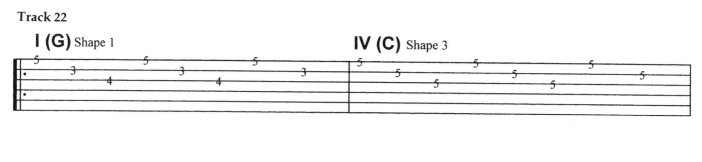

You should be practicing all these arpeggios on your three bass strings as well.

The relationship between these shapes never change no matter what key you are playing in. So lets try a couple of other keys. I am only going to give you the starting places for this, just follow the same patterns and you will be playing the correct arpeggios for the I IV and V chords in each key.

Key of E

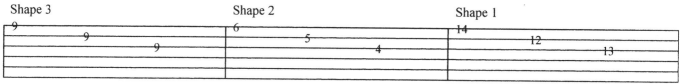

Practice playing through these arpeggios in other keys as well.

3 Minor Arpeggio Shapes

Here are the 3 G minor arpeggio shapes on the dobro neck.

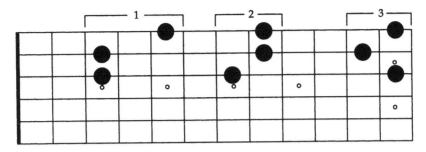

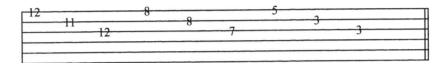

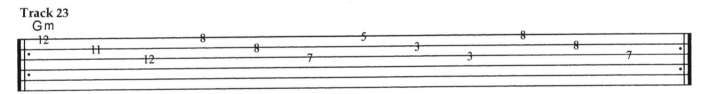

Lets play through these minor arpeggios.

Track 23
Gm

Now lets play through the (more often used) minor arpeggios of Em and Am.

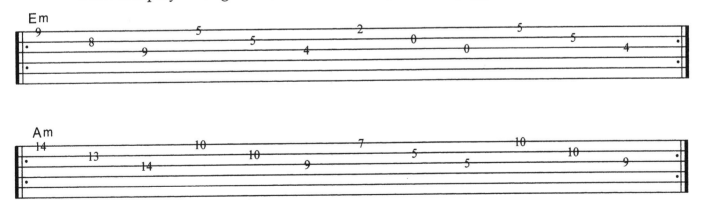

31

Now lets do the same thing we did with the major arpeggios and run through the I, IV, V chord progression for the key of E minor, using each of the 3 minor shapes as our staring point. * Take Note – Usually when you play in a minor key, the I and IV chords are minor and the V chord is major. We will play our arpeggios with this in mind… (using Em, Am, B arpeggios).

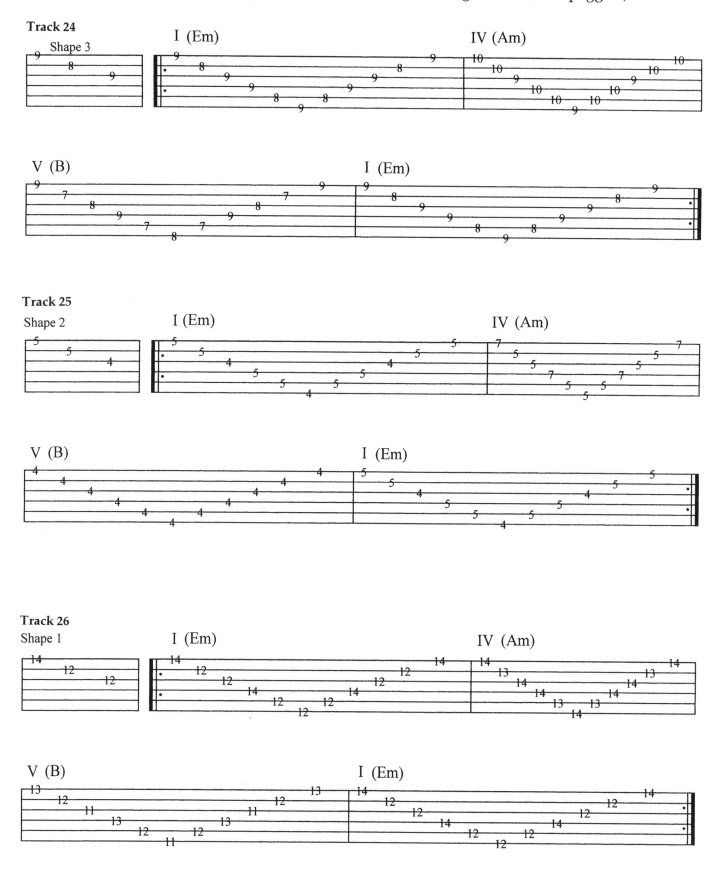

Track 24
Shape 3   I (Em)   IV (Am)

V (B)   I (Em)

Track 25
Shape 2   I (Em)   IV (Am)

V (B)   I (Em)

Track 26
Shape 1   I (Em)   IV (Am)

V (B)   I (Em)

Lets do the same set of patterns in the key of Am.

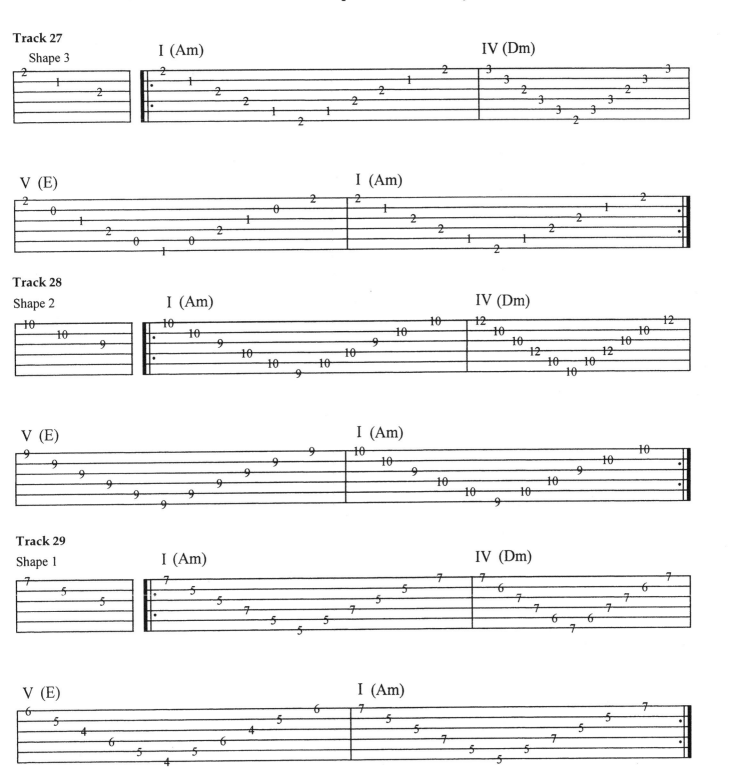

Now, run all the shapes together for each chord.

Track 30

I (Am)

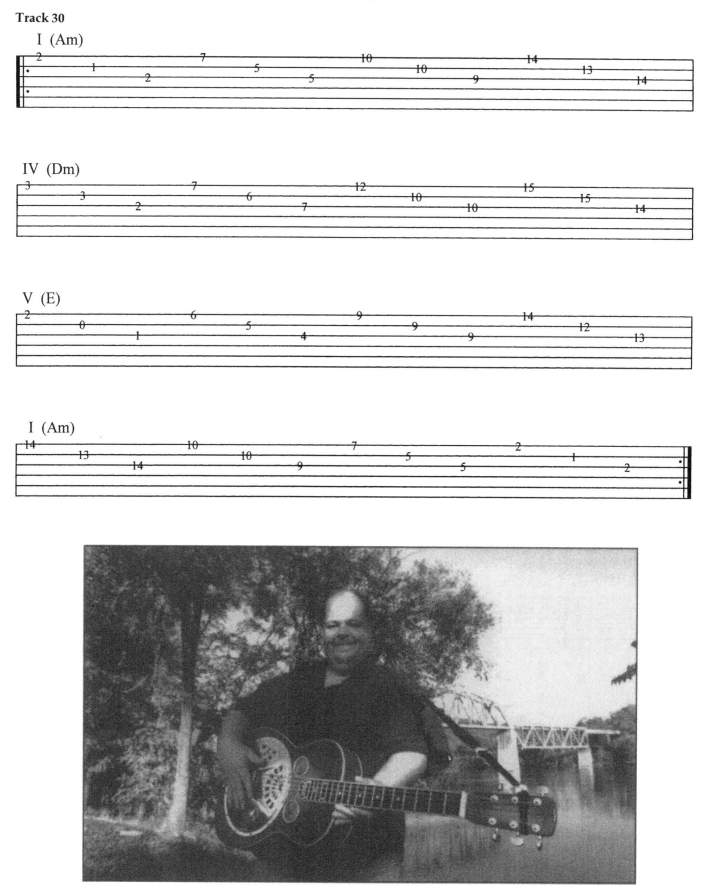

IV (Dm)

V (E)

I (Am)

Phil Leadbetter

Make sure you don't get stuck with only playing these arpeggios on your treble strings. Try this one the bass strings as well.

Track 31

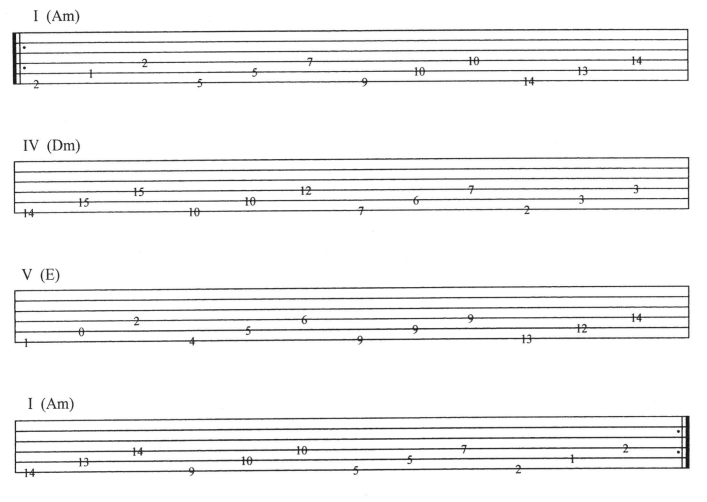

Norm Hamlet

We are now going to look at chords made up of 4 notes, starting with the 7th chord. As mentioned in the previous chord construction chart, the 7th chord (also called the dominant 7th) makes use of the flat 7th in relation to the 7th degree of the major scale.

The flat 7th is always 2 frets behind the root note on your instrument. This means if you can find your root notes, just go back 2 frets and you will also easily find the flat 7th!

We are going to learn a 7th chord arpeggio pattern off of root notes on each string.

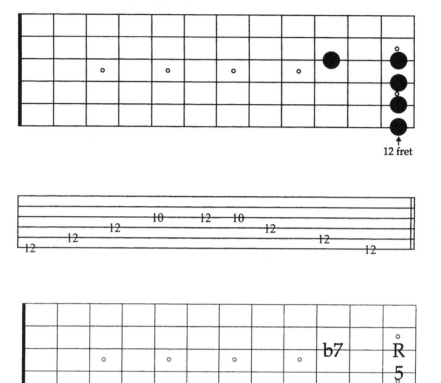

Lets play through a simple 12 bar blues in the Key of G using the arpeggio we just learned in the G7, C7 and D7 positions.

Track 32

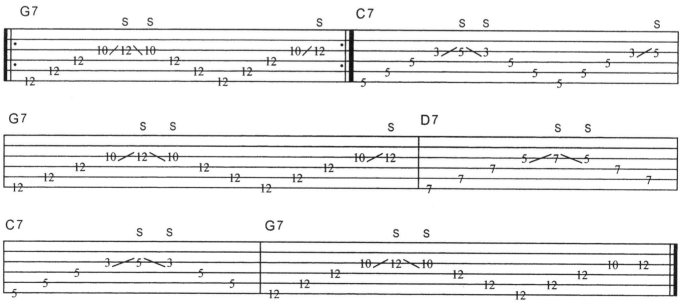

36

Here's another arpeggio pattern you can run off the Root note on the 3rd and 1st strings.

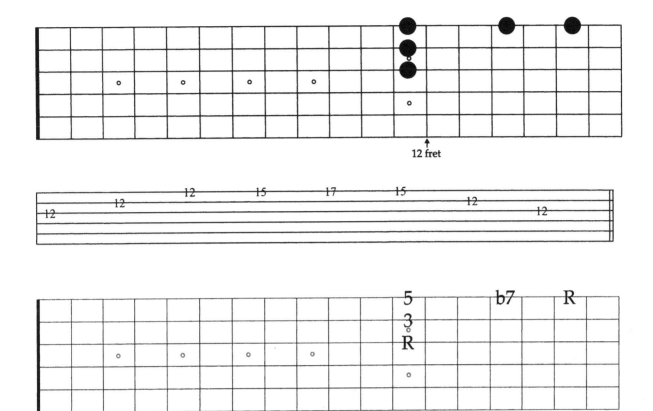

12 fret

Blues in G

Let's play through the same pattern as last time using the new arpeggio.

Track 33

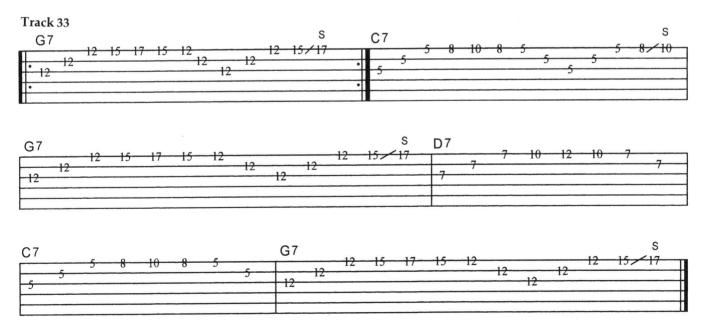

37

Now, let's do the same thing with the 7th chords built off Roots notes on the other strings.

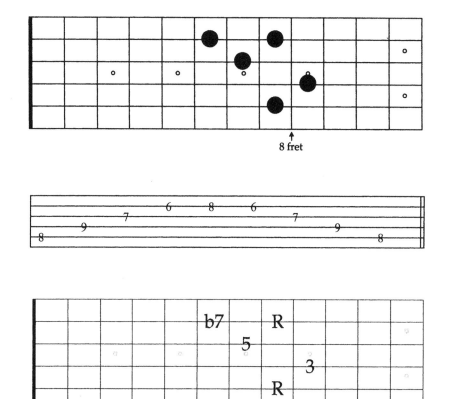

↑
8 fret

Blues in G

Track 34

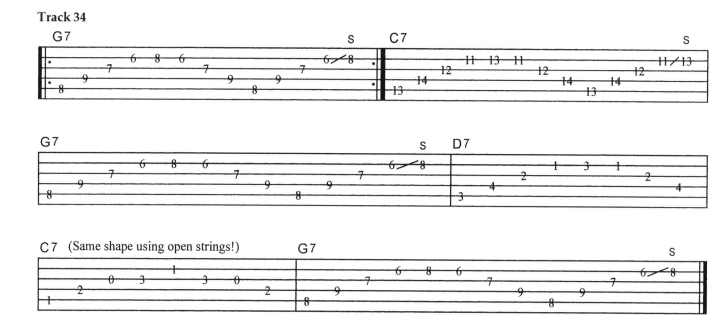

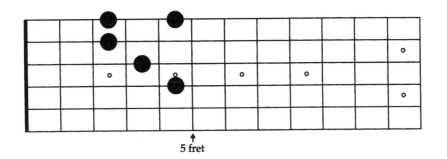

5 fret

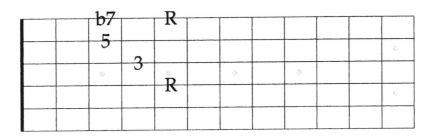

Blues in G

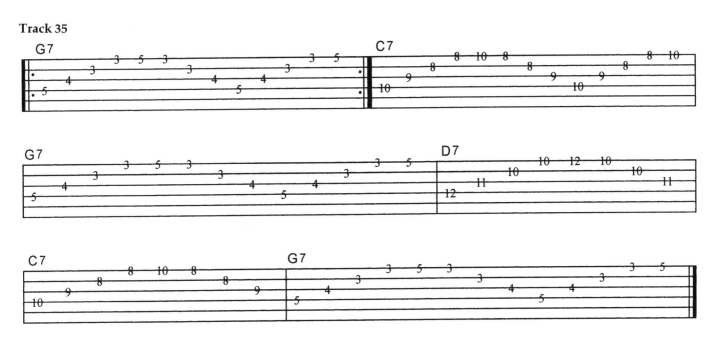

39

Let's tie these 7th arpeggio shapes together through the I, IV, V chord progression. By now, you are likely getting a little tired of the key of G. Let's move to the key of E for these next exercises…same shapes… different key! Find those root notes for the key of E on each string before you start.

Blues in E

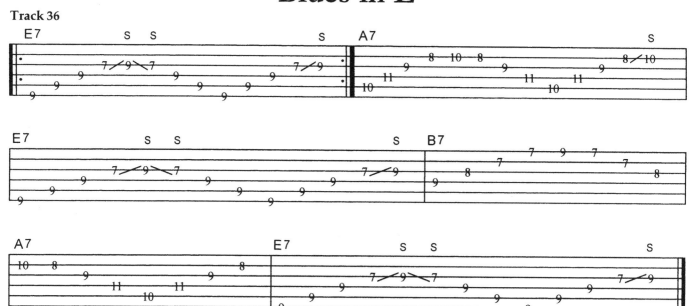

Blues in E

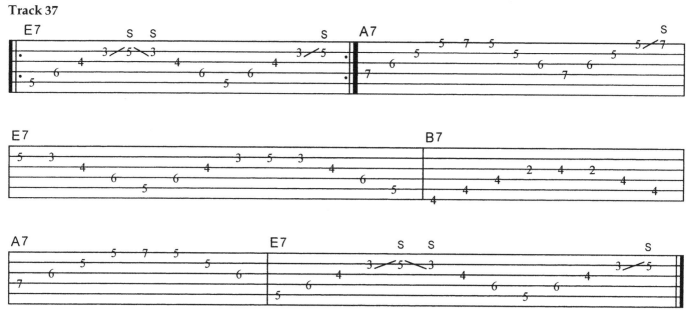

Blues in E

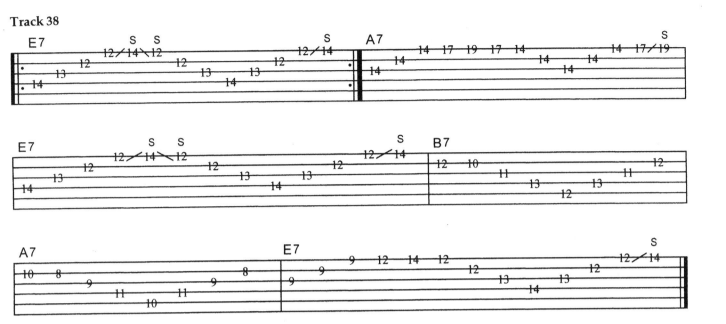

Cindy Cashdollar

Photo: Scott Newton

41

The minor 7th chord shapes are the same as the 7th chord shapes only in each case, you lower (flatten) the third degree of the scale.

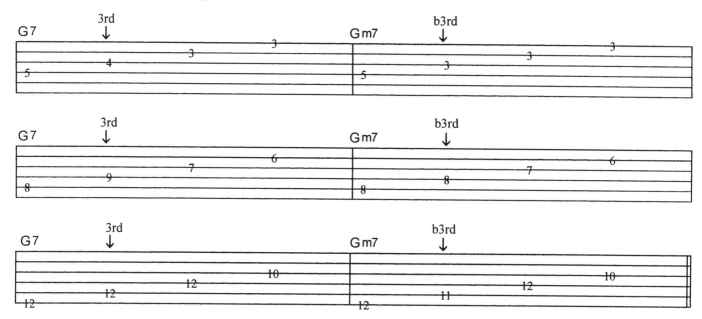

Note how each of these arpeggios only have one note changed in them (the 3rd is flattened, making them minor arpeggios)
play through each of the minor 7th arpeggios until you are comfortable with them.

We are going to practice our minor 7th arpeggios by playing over top of the standard minor 7th I chord to dominant 7th IV chord progression popular in Latin music (a-la Santana) and other styles as well...

note – if you really want to get inside of your arpeggios (to the point where you can use them at anytime) make sure to pay attention to what degree of the scale you are playing at all times. This will train your ear, help you get to know your instrument and most importantly, teach you which harmony notes are the ones that you like best. Most musicians seem to have particular harmony notes that they favour and this helps define their style of playing. You will also discover that certain harmony notes are favoured in different styles of music.

Track 39

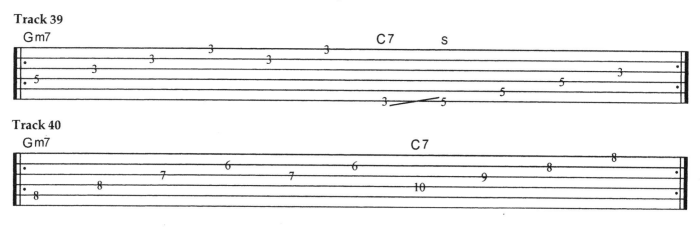

Track 40

Track 41

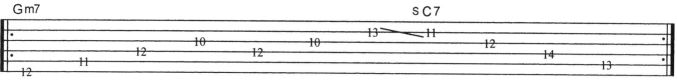

Track 42

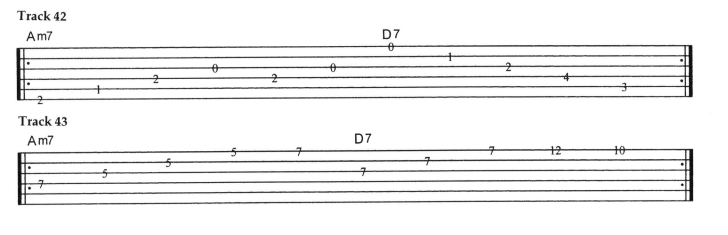

Track 43

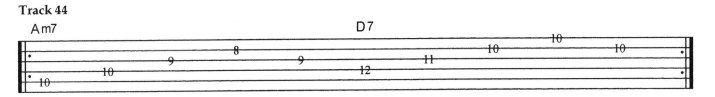

Track 44

Mike Auldridge
Photo: John Lee

note- how our first example here makes use of open strings.

Lets also try the ever-popular I, vim7, iim7, V7 (also called 1, 6, 2, 5) chord progression with arpegios through each of them.

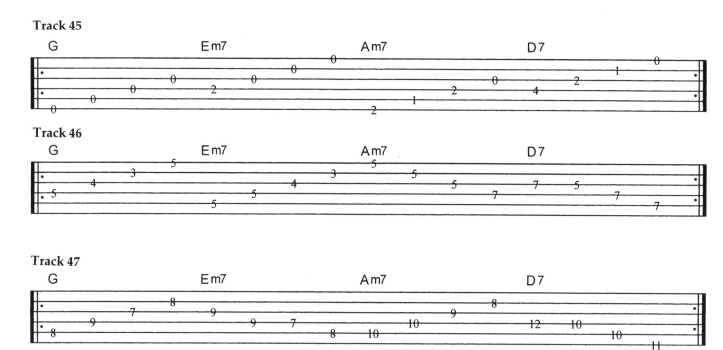

again, note the open strings in the first example. Try
to see the shapes even though we are using open strings!

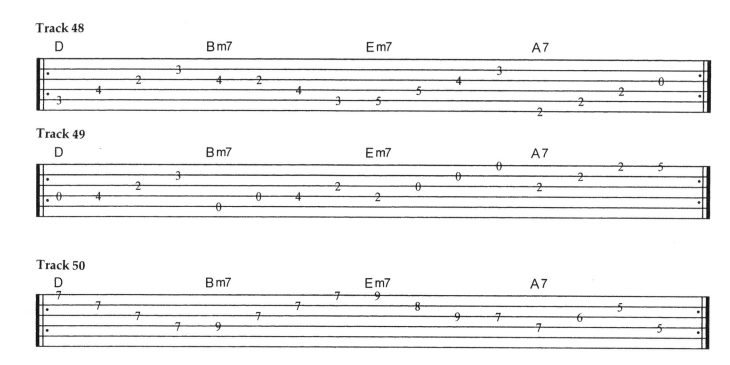

The Major 7th

The other type of 7th chord to arpeggiate (is that a word?)... is the major 7th. This chord consists of the 7th that fits with the major scale and I jokingly refer to it as the 'sensitive new-age guy chord'. You hear it lots in the hits of 70's and 80's bands like America and Air Supply. Used with discretion, the major 7th is a very sweet sounding chord.

Shape 1

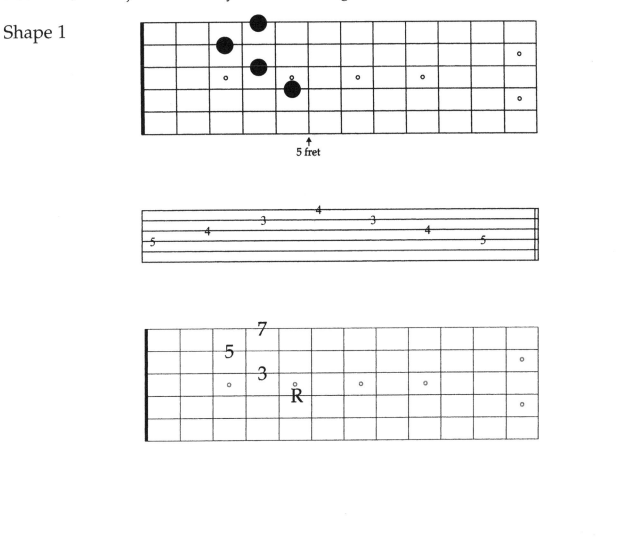

5 fret

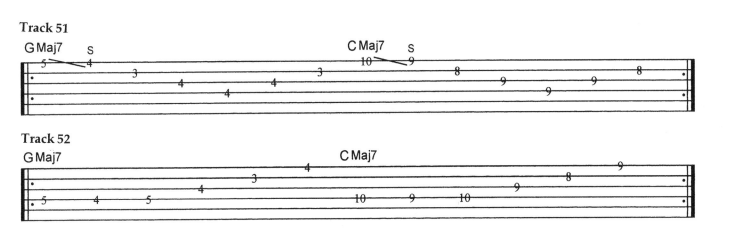

Track 51
G Maj7   S   C Maj7   S

Track 52
G Maj7   C Maj7

45

Shape 2

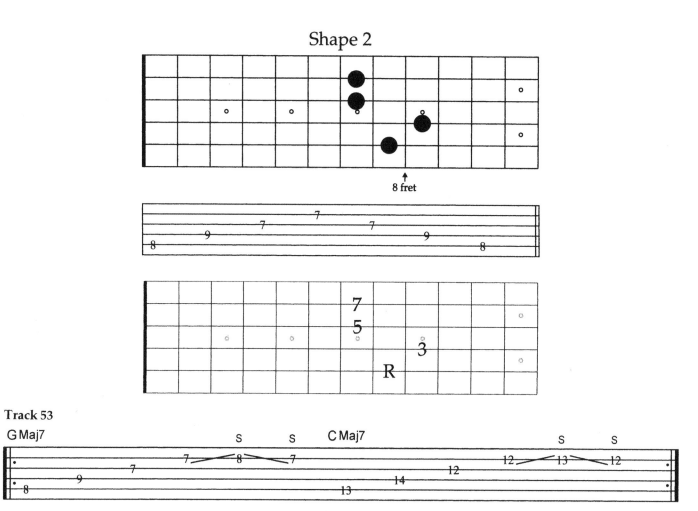

↑
8 fret

Track 53

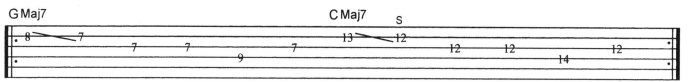

Track 54

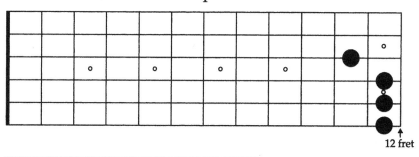

Shape 3

↑
12 fret

Track 55

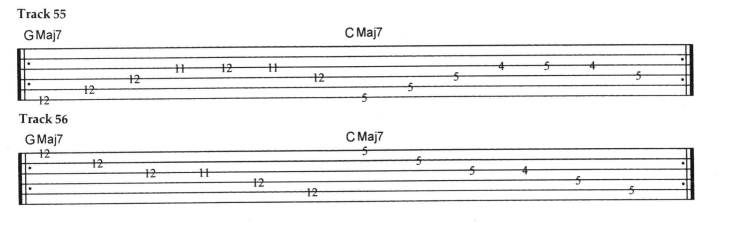

Track 56

Lets put all the major 7th arpeggios together

Track 57

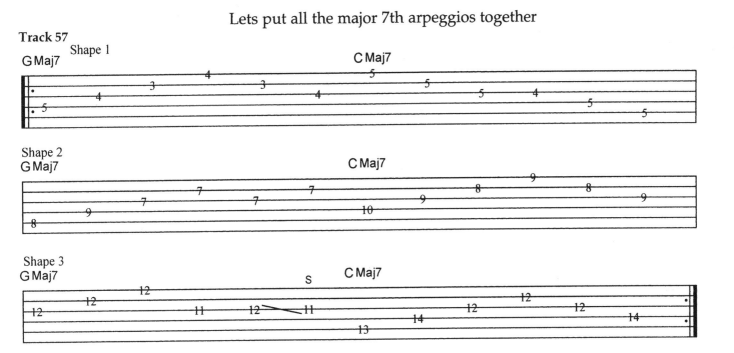

Conclusion

Congratulations, you have made it through book 1. You should be feeling comfortable at this point with the major scales, the major and minor arpeggios and the different types of 7th chords. You should also be starting to hear the difference between major and minor as well as 7ths. You are well on your way to becoming an improvising Dobro player at this point and hopefully, you will take this information and begin bravely jamming with others whenever you get the chance. In the next book, we will explore all the other types of chords there are and how they fit into different styles of music. Until then, *enjoy your playing* and see ya on the road!

Doug Cox